Founding Sponsor
SELFRIDGES&C⁰

So Special

by Kevin Hood

Welcome to The Studio – the Royal Exchange's new venue dedicated to the theatre of the future. This is a space for innovation and discovery, imagination and daring.

It's a space in which you can encounter the voices that will shape the theatre of tomorrow and where we can promote young talent and build new audiences for the millennium and beyond.

Designer Laurie Dennett has devised a theatrical box of tricks equipped for multiple uses with flexible seating. With its atmospheric shades of blue and unique spatial possibilities, it inspires incoming artists with a challenge very different from that of the empty black box that constitutes the second space in most other theatres.

In our first season of work here the Royal Exchange presents four world premières, including work by début playwrights and the first results of our new policy of commissioning theatre for children and young people. We are also playing host to a brilliant selection of the most exciting touring companies from Britain and abroad, high calibre practitioners who specialise in a diverse array of styles and genres of performance. You'll find new stories being told here, as well as new ways of telling stories.

You will also find a constant buzz of educational workshops and other activities and events related to the work we do. Why not check out our Live Trailers, where you can get a taste for the forthcoming show from short, sharp cameo readings by the actors intercut with soundbites from the author. Or – another first in theatre – try out the 12 track in the foyer, where you can punch out a juke box selection of music or soundscape from the current show.

In this space a long standing dream has become a reality. At the new Royal Exchange there are other dreams that have come true, in the renewal of the building as well as in our programme of work, but in the Studio we would like the realisation of the dream to remain a little dream-like – a place of uncanny surprises and seductive strangeness, in which the unthinkable can be thought.

Matthew Lloyd
Artistic Director, November 1998

The **Studio**

- The Royal Exchange's **new** studio is right next to the 750-seat theatre inside the newly-transformed Royal Exchange building.

- A totally **flexible** space seating up to 120 with its own foyer, bar and **sound installation**.

- Dedicated to the theatre of the **future**.

- Presenting . . .

    the **best** new voices in British playwriting

    the most **exciting** national and international work for young people

    the most **innovative** touring theatre companies working today.

- A full programme of

    Workshops

    Conversations and

    Special Events for those who want to find out about and be a part of the world of theatre.

- The newest addition to Manchester's **vibrant** cultural scene.

- An **experience** in blue . . . blue for **imagination** and **dreams**.

Welcome.

Enjoy.

The Studio

Opening Season 1998–99

SO SPECIAL   **3 Dec – 19 Dec 1998**
by Kevin Hood, directed by Matthew Lloyd

Visiting company   **21 Dec – 2 Jan 1999**
Pop Up Theatre Company
SNOW SHOES
by Michael Dalton

Visiting company   **28 Jan – 30 Jan 1999**
Frantic Assembly
SELL-OUT
by Michael Wynne, choreographer T.C. Howard

Visiting company   **5 – 6 Feb 1999**
Bouge De-Là's
EVOLUTION: BODY
devised by the company

THE RIB CAGE   **17 Feb – 13 March 1999**
by Nicola Baldwin, directed by Gordon Anderson

FAST FOOD   **24 March –10 April 1999**
by Abi Morgan, directed by Marianne Elliott

CAFÉ VESUVIO **21 April – 8 May 1999**
by Nona Shepphard, directed by Nona Shepphard

Visiting company **8 – 12 June 1999**
People Show No. 107
created and devised by the company,
directed by David Terence

Visiting company **15 – 19 June 1999**
Compagnie Gare Centrale
PETITES FABLES
by Agnès Limbos,
directed by Agnès Limbos and François Bloch

Visiting company **7 – 10 July 1999**
The Fittings Group and Graeae Theatre
FITTINGS
by Mike Kenny,
directed by Garry Robson and Jenny Sealey

Royal Exchange Theatre
St Ann's Square, Manchester M2 7DH

Box Office: 0161 833 9833

So Special

An Introduction

Teenage pregnancy, broken homes, kids in care, on drugs, at odds with the system – the stuff of a thousand 'Issue-Dramas'. But, as Porsh says, 'I am not that cliché. That is not who I am.' The play transcends the stereotypes that make up its starting-point by allowing its characters to be the driving force of the drama – not their problems or deprivations, not the external facts of their life, but what comes from inside them, their imagination and their language. It's in the verbal scrapping that, instinctively, they find their survival kit and their escape route, their favourite drug and their most unlicensed weapon. And with Porsh, because (as she is sarcastically aware) she's special, it goes further still – a blistering articulacy, true to her own life on the street and studded with brilliant magpie additions, which draws strength and anger and wit all the time from the stereotyping that gives her the priceless edge of surprise.

Matthew Lloyd
Artistic Director

The Studio, Royal Exchange Theatre
presents the world première of

Special

by Kevin Hood

PORSH	Sharon Duncan Brewster
KAREN	Emily Jane Aston
MOTHER / SONIA / NURSE	Claire Benedict
SAM	Lee Oakes
TOMMY	Edward Purver

Director	Matthew Lloyd
Assistant Director	George Ormond
Designer	Liz Ascroft
Lighting	Kevin Sleep
Sound	Steve Morgan

Company Manager	Louise Tischler
Stage Manager	Louise Ormerod
Deputy Stage Manager	Harry Teale

With thanks to: Blockbuster Video, Mary Brennan and staff at St. Mary's Hospital, Rosemary Connor at Trafford Healthcare NHS Trust.

First performed December 3rd 1998 at
The Studio, Royal Exchange Theatre, Manchester.
Press night December 8th.

Biographies

KEVIN HOOD (Writer)

Kevin was born and raised in Durham. He studied science at both the University of Newcastle and University College London. He went on to spend six years working in medical research and then nine years teaching. He now lives in South East London.

He has written extensively for television and his credits include GRANGE HILL, EASTENDERS and MEDICS. He wrote the four lead episodes of SILENT WITNESS for the BBC, for which he was recently awarded the tenth Recontres Européennes de Télévision de Reims for Best Script. He also wrote the Channel 4 TV film WORK.

His plays include PHOTOSTORY for the Hampstead Theatre; HAMMET'S APPRENTICE for the Royal Court Theatre. For the Warehouse Theatre he wrote SUGAR HILL BLUES (toured to Hampstead Theatre and produced for radio), THE ASTRONOMER'S GARDEN (also toured to the Royal Court) and BEACHED. He also wrote THE FENCE (Albany Empire and Edinburgh Festival Fringe).

Kevin is under contract to the RSC and is currently writing IN A LAND OF PLENTY, a ten-part serial for BBC2 to be broadcast in Spring 2000, as well as a film for Ecosse Films.

CLAIRE BENEDICT (Mother / Sonia / Nurse)
trained at LAMDA and was previously seen at the Royal Exchange in DEATH AND THE KING'S HORSEMAN and MEDEA. Other theatre credits include MOON ON A RAINBOW SHAWL (Almeida) for which she won the Time Out award for Best Actress; FLASH TRASH (Half Moon Theatre); KING OF ENGLAND (Theatre Royal, Stratford East); SO LONG ON LONELY STREET (Palace Theatre, Watford); THE WHITE DEVIL (Royal National Theatre);

ODYSSEY, ANTONY AND CLEOPATRA and TAMBURLAINE THE GREAT (Royal Shakespeare Company); VICTOR AND THE LADIES (Tricycle Theatre) and A MIDSUMMER NIGHT'S DREAM (English Shakespeare Company). Radio work includes KYRNON'S KINGDOM, MORGAN'S CAY, YOU MAY LEAVE, THE SHOW IS OVER, A MIDSUMMER NIGHT'S DREAM and THE ORESTEIA (BBC World Service); INVISIBLE CITIES (BBC Radio 3) and CHARLIE TANGO, DEATH AND THE KING'S HORSEMAN, RAINMAKER, A RAISIN IN SUN, UNITED STATES, A SONG OF A BLUE FOOT, SPELL NUMBER 7 and DILEMMAS (BBC Radio 4). Television work has included THE BILL, PRIME SUSPECT, TEXT IN TIME, CALL RED, GRANGE HILL, DREAM TEAM and, as part of the 'Windrush' season, STILL HERE: JUST SO MUCH A BODY CAN TAKE. Films include SEASICK, THE FIFTH PROVINCE and, most recently, FELICIA'S JOURNEY.

SHARON DUNCAN-BREWSTER (Porsh)
trained at the Anna Scher Theatre School. Her previous theatre credits include BABIES and ASHES AND SAND (Royal Court Upstairs); NO BOYS CRICKETS CLUB (Theatre Royal Stratford East); a touring production of CAUGHT IN THE ACT; YARD GIRLS (Royal Court and on tour) and CRAVE (Paines Plough). Radio work includes TOKOLOSH and television credits include TO HAVE AND TO HOLD, STARTING OUT, UP THE GARDEN PATH, 2.4 CHILDREN, GRANGE HILL, EASTENDERS, BETWEEN THE LINES, HOPE I DIE BEFORE I GET OLD, KING OF HEARTS, CHRISTMAS, BACKUP, FIRST SIGHT, THE BILL and MAISIE RAINE. Films include STRONG KIDS SAFE KIDS and BODY STORY.

EMILY JANE ASTON (Jane)
has previous theatre credits which include HEADLAND and A GHOST FROM A PERFECT PLACE (Bolton Octagon). Television work includes THE WEIRDSTONE OF BRISINGAMMON, THINK ABOUT SCIENCE, CASUALTY, THE BILL, CHILDREN'S WARD, COVINGTON CROSS, ORANGES

ARE NOT THE ONLY FRUIT, GROWING PAINS, HEARTBEAT and CORONATION STREET. Films include BUTTERFLY KISS.

LEE OAKES (Sam)
has theatre credits which include ALL OF YOU MINE (Bush Theatre). His television credits include THE LIVER BIRDS, CASUALTY, THE LAKES, DANGERFIELD and THE GIRLIE SKETCH SHOW. Films include DRAGONHEART, DAYLIGHT, FORK IN THE ROAD, DANNY'S STORY and MILK.

EDWARD PURVER (Tommy)
trained at LAMDA and has previous theatre credits which include MOJO (Bristol New Vic); PETER PAN (West Yorkshire Playhouse) and THE SOLDIER'S TALE (Theatre Artaud). Television work includes A TOUCH OF FROST, DANGERFIELD, THE BILL, THE GRAND, TRIAL AND RETRIBUTION, TRAUMA and SOLDIER SOLDIER. Films include ELIZABETH.

MATTHEW LLOYD (Director)
is an Artistic Director of the Royal Exchange Theatre Company, where he has previously directed AN EXPERIENCED WOMAN GIVES ADVICE by Iain Heggie, ALL'S WELL THAT ENDS WELL, THE ILLUSION, PRESENT LAUGHTER and most recently the award-winning AN EXPERIMENT WITH AN AIR-PUMP. He was previously an Associate Director at Hampstead Theatre where his directorial credits include the multi-award-winning THE FASTEST CLOCK IN THE UNIVERSE, LION IN THE STREETS, A GOING CONCERN, GHOST FROM A PERFECT PLACE, THE MAIDEN STONE, SLAVS! by Tony Kushner, THE ELEVENTH COMMANDMENT, APOCALYPTICA and most recently the London transfer of AN EXPERIMENT WITH AN AIR-PUMP. His many other theatre credits include DEATHWATCH and MEASURE FOR MEASURE off Broadway; DEMOCRACY at the Gate Theatre;

2 SAMUEL II etc at the Royal Court Upstairs: THE HOME SHOW PIECES and LA RONDE for Glasgow Citizens; THE PITCHFORK DISNEY at the Bush Theatre; THE LA PLAYS at the Almeida Theatre: CLOUD 9 at the Parko Theatre, Tokyo and A MIDSUMMER NIGHT'S DREAM at Leicester Haymarket. Opera credits include THE BARBER OF SEVILLE for Scottish-Opera-Go-Round. Future projects include DREAMING by Peter Barnes and WAITING FOR GODOT with Richard Wilson, both at the Royal Exchange in 1999.

LIZ ASCROFT (Designer)
decided to become a designer whilst attending her first summer course at Manchester Youth Theatre. Three summers later she went on to train at Wimbledon School of Art. After graduating she spent a year on an Arts Council Bursary at the Belgrade Theatre, Coventry. Liz has been Designer In Residence at Liverpool Everyman, Plymouth Theatre Royal and the Wolsey Theatre in Ipswich. She has worked freelance for, amongst others, the Duke's Theatre, Lancaster; Hull Truck Theatre Company, the Northcott, Exeter; Solent People's Theatre Company, the Women's Theatre Group and Hampstead Theatre. Favourite productions include THE MAN IN THE MOON, TROJAN WOMEN, and 'TIS PITY SHE'S A WHORE (Liverpool Everyman), GRAPES OF WRATH (R.A.D.A.). HOLDING THE REINS (Women's Theatre Group), ZOLA'S EARTH (Cheltenham Everyman), DEATH AND THE MAIDEN, ALICE'S ADVENTURES IN WONDERLAND, A MIDSUMMER NIGHT'S DREAM (Dukes, Lancaster) and APOCALYPTICA (Hampstead Theatre). Most recently Liz has designed KATHERINE HOWARD and NEVILLE'S ISLAND at the Dukes, Lancaster.

KEVIN SLEEP (Lighting Designer)
has regularly lit shows in the West End among which his favourites remain the award-winning THE HOUSE OF BERNARDO ALBA , BLUES IN THE NIGHT, PRIN, EARTHA KITT IN CONCERT, DEATH AND THE MAIDEN and the long

running WOMAN IN BLACK. His previous work for the Royal Exchange includes ROAD, THE WINTER'S TALE, VENICE PRESERVED, I HAVE BEEN HERE BEFORE and THE ROAD TO MECCA. His other extensive theatre credits include THE WICKED OLD MAN and BURNING EVEREST for West Yorkshire Playhouse; VOLPONE, GHOSTS, WHOSE AFRAID OF VIRGINIA WOLF? and THE CRUICIBLE at the Royal Lyceum, Edinburgh; THE BROWNING VERSION, CEASAR AND CLEOPATRA, THE LAST WALTZ and UNDER THE STARS at Greenwich; THE BOYS FROM SYRACUSE, THE GOVERNMENT INSPECTOR, THE TAMING OF THE SHREW and THE WIZARD OF OZ at the Sheffield Crucible; JOCK TAMSEN'S BAIRNS and CARMEN for Communicado Theatre Company; THE MAN OF MODE and THE LIBERTINE for Out of Joint Theatre Company at the Royal Court; the PITLOCHRY FESTIVAL THEATRE SEASONS 1992–1996; ROUGH JUSTICE and PAINTING CHURCHES for the Nuffield Theatre, Southampton; ROMEO AND JULIET at the Sherman Theatre, Cardiff; THE OLD DEVILS.

STEVE MORGAN (Sound) is a composer, improviser, DJ and sound designer. Recent theatre projects include OUTSIDE ON THE STREET and LEONCE AND LENA both at the Gate Theatre, London. Also an interactive soundtrack for Ionesco's L'OEUF DUR produced by Bonbo, an Anglo-French theatre company which he co-founded. He collaborates with artist Shane Waltener in producing sound and sculpture installations, and devises site-specific club events with performance and visual arts elements. He has written theme and incidental music for television including ROUGH GUIDE for BBC 2 and THE WORD for Channel 4 as well as music for animated shorts. He was the keyboard player for Manchester-based big-band funk outfit FRANTIC and more recently has recorded originals and remixes as part of drum'n'bass act SPACEK.

Kevin Hood
So Special

First published in 1998
by Faber and Faber Limited
3 Queen Square, London WC1N 3AU

Typeset by Country Setting, Kingsdown, Kent CT14 8ES
Printed in England by Intype London Ltd

All rights reserved

© Kevin Hood, 1998

Kevin Hood is hereby identified as author
of this work in accordance with Section 77 of the
Copyright, Designs and Patents Act 1988

All rights whatsoever in this work are strictly reserved.
Applications for permission for any use whatsoever
including performance rights must be made in advance, prior
to any such proposed use, to Judy Daish Associates,
2 St Charles Place, London W10 6EG No performance
may be given unless a licence has first been obtained.

This book is sold subject to the condition that it shall not, by way
of trade or otherwise, be lent, resold, hired out or otherwise
circulated without the publisher's prior consent in any form of
binding or cover other than that in which it is published and
without a similar condition including this condition being
imposed on the subsequent purchaser

A CIP record for this book
is available from the British Library

ISBN 0-571-20044-3

2 4 6 8 10 9 7 5 3 1

Characters

Porsh
Late teens. Mixed race. Londoner. Fast talker.
Always wears enormous, brutal boots.

Karen
Mid-teens. White. Lancashire.

Sam
Late teens. White.
Londoner with a twist of Al Pacino.

Tommy
Early twenties. Doctor. White. Home counties.

Mother
Forties. Black. Jamaican–English.

Sonia
Forties. Black. English. Middle-class accent.

Nurse
Forties. Black.

Act One

SCENE ONE

Hospital grounds.
Porsh and Karen, both nine months pregnant, are sitting on a bench. Porsh is filling in a form. Karen tunes her radio.

Porsh Everyone has their own plan, and place.

Karen I haven't. I haven't got nowhere, except me Dad's and he won't have me back, the bastard.

Porsh I mean in their own life.

Karen Cunt.

Porsh But if something goes wrong with that plan and a person gets pushed out of their place – well it int just them, it int that simple, 'cos the next person along gets pushed out too. And next person along from them, suddenly it comes over her that . . .

Karen What?

Porsh That . . . everything is wrong, man.

Karen How come?

Porsh Just comes over her.

Karen But how?

Porsh *And* over the next one. So on and so forth till the entire situ-a-tion is complete dev-ast-a-tion.

Karen 'Dev-ast-a-tion.'

Porsh Des-o-la-tion.

Karen 'Des-o-la-tion.'

Porsh Something has to be done, man.

Karen Has to be.

Karen tunes a blast on the radio.

Porsh (*reads*) Date of birth. Date of birth. Date of birth.

The radio goes dead.

(*Throws pen down.*) Thing about me is I'm not who I am.

Karen I dunt get it.

Porsh My birthday is *wrong*. Just 'cos she said it was like '*this*' day does not *make* it like '*this*' day it just makes it what she *said*.

Karen We talking about your mother?

Porsh My mother's dead.

Karen (*delight*) Mine too. What about your Dad?

Porsh He was a dick.

Karen And mine's a cunt. Gerron then, wunt they?

Porsh I mean that's all he ever was. Some dick.

Karen Oh.

Porsh Dreamed about him – it – once. Big dick daddy.

Karen Fookin' batteries! Dead fookin' *shite*!

Karen throws old batteries away and fits new.

Porsh And she lied about my birthday.

Karen Why?

Porsh Just did. I know it, man.

Karen How?

Porsh It come over me.

Karen Yeah . . . Yeah, but . . . worrabout your certificate?

Porsh She lied on it.

Karen And worrabout your stars?

Porsh Pisces!

Karen (*delight*) Me an' all.

Porsh Crossed up, fucked up and *well* out of who I'm supposed to be, innit. Pisces! Never felt right.

Karen Why?

Porsh Because it int really me. Me, I'm somebody else altogether. Please please *please* let me be somebody else altogether.

She goes back to filling in the form.

Date of birth.

Karen Talk, dunt ya?

Porsh 'S why I get Porsh. Fast. Like me. Brum brum. Porsh.

Karen Look, you're goin' too fast –

Porsh My first word was helicopter. Amazing.

Karen Still are.

Porsh Yeah. And chicken, chicken, chicken, relax. Gonna look after you.

Karen Yer will?

Porsh Course I fookin' won't.

They both laugh. Karen plugs in her radio – and lucks into something good. They drag themselves to their feet. They dance. The Nurse comes on, stands, hands on hips and stares.

Nurse You two! I'd hoped to keep you two apart.

Karen Sorry, miss.

Porsh Miss Nursy.

The Nurse turns off the radio.

Karen Miss miss.

Porsh Nursy nursy.

Nurse looks one to the other.

Nurse Uh huh!

The Nurse goes.

Karen *Porsh!*

Porsh Also Porsh as in Portia as in *The Merchant of Venice.*

Pause.

Karen Hate Geography. Teacher wouldn't have me in lesson 'cos I stuck this compass in her leg when everybody was crowded round the desk. Couldn't prove *nowt.* But she knew it were me so I got suspended any road. Went septic. Her leg.

Porsh Chopped off?

Karen No.

Porsh Pity.

Porsh snaps the radio back on, very loud. The Nurse comes rapidly on.

Nurse Will you turn that noise down!

Porsh No.

Nurse Will you *turn* that –

Porsh We're enjoyin' it!

Porsh holds the radio away from the Nurse – who nevertheless gets it. And turns it down.

Nurse You're disturbing the other patients.

Karen So we shouldn't enjoy ourselves now, is that it?

Nurse Would have thought you two had done enough 'enjoying' already.

Pause, then:

Karen and **Porsh** (*mocking*) Ooooooooo!

Nurse Girls! Now, girls. Now you just listen to me, girls –

Karen and **Porsh** Ooooooooo!

Nurse There are some very ill people here.

Porsh Int them mind.

Karen They don't mind.

Porsh It's you that *minds*.

Nurse Just keep it down or I'll take it away.

Karen blows a huge bubble. Pops it. Porsh sucks tooth at the Nurse – who goes.

Porsh (*shouts after*) Slag park!

Karen (*shouting after*) Love girls!

Karen and **Porsh** (*unexpectedly together*) Crackface!

Mutual amazement. They have another go.

Hospitals!

And another.

Porsh FUCKIN' DUMP!

Karen FOOKIN' DUMP!

Karen and **Porsh** Nurses!

Karen And she's worst bloody bastard bitch of the lot!

Porsh You seen *Thelma and Louise*?

Karen What ward they in, then?

Porsh (*laughs*) *The film*! So, what's your name?

Karen Karen. Burr I get Kar.

Porsh Porsh but it's Ruth really. And how you get yourself in here, chicken?

Karen Hoppin' off school. Missed out on things like Science an' all that that that . . . you know. Missed everything. Except flowering plants. And invertebrates.

Porsh No boners.

Karen Yer what?

Porsh Don't matter, we didn't do dicks neither.

Karen You didn't do them in mammals?

Porsh No, we did mammals in general. Characteristics: mammary glands, fur, tails –

Karen Where's that?

Porsh (*points*) Bone here called the coccyx – tails, tits, live young but no dicks, not a furry dick in sight – not worth lookin' at anyway. So you didn't know all that like useful information then?

Pause.

Karen We had this film once: flowers wavin' them . . . things all over t'place, them . . .

Porsh Stamens.

Karen Things with pollen all over t'shop and if that weren't a warnin' don't know what fookin' was. Invertebrates – yuck! – dead disgustin'. *Beans*, though – now yer fookin' talkin'!

Pause.

Porsh I mean what got you here specifically?

Karen Heart murmur. Me Dad says I get it from me Mum but I reckon I were born that way.

Porsh What does your Mum say?

Karen Dunno. Never met her. When I were little, used to think it were her – murmurin' in me heart. Gorra fag?

Porsh No.

Karen Dunt ya?

Porsh Come on! I lived in a children's home.

Karen Well then?

Porsh produces a spliff.

Porsh Puff?

Karen Oh. 'K you.

They smoke.

We stuck them like . . . between this like –

Porsh Don't get you?

Karen Beans! Two of them. Between blotting paper rolled-up into a tube and this glass . . . jar . . . tube with exactly one inch of water in the bottom and no more else it rots the bean. The idea is water soaks up t'keep them moist. I *were* careful, it weren't my fault, fookin' bean fell in all by itself. And then something got into it. And then it didn't work no more. So I were left wi' just the one. And then you have to wait . . .

Porsh Till?

Karen This long lumpy thing starts in the top. Under t'skin. Bulgy. Like a stiffy.

Porsh Beans don't get stiffies.

Karen How it looked. And then skin splits and this like white thing (*acts it*) un un un . . .

Porsh Coils.

Karen No.

Porsh Unfurls.

Karen Swishes out – two little smooth greeny whitey thingies openin' out their like what you might think are leaves only they're not 'cos they're something else apparently.

Porsh Cotyledons.

Karen Coty . . . Coty . . . Come again?

Porsh Cotyledons. Leaves come after apparently. Furly.

Pause.

So what happened next?

Karen It dropped in t'water and fookin' teacher got me suspended.

Porsh What for?

Karen Burned his hand wi' an 'ot test tube.

Porsh Oh. So you never found out.

Karen No. Worrabout you?

Porsh Well in my case it wasn't beans it was nipples.

Pause.

Karen Dunt get you.

Porsh It was like this.

Porsh cuts the lights with an imaginary remote control.

SCENE TWO

Sam and Porsh, stoned, in a heap of videos at the back of video shop.

Sam Look, the story hasn't even started, but it's already over. The future has happened.

Porsh And what about *Terminator Two*? Terminator came back from the future to do something about it. What about Sarah Connor and the freedom fighters not *letting* the machines rule the Earth? And brave and cleverness make no difference?

Sam I'm just saying it was supposed to happen and it did.

Porsh No such thing as supposed to happen. Not if you've got a plan.

Sam Don't get that.

Porsh That you have to make happen. You start in the cold and dark and walk.

Sam Start where?

Porsh On the moon.

Sam *Where?*

Porsh We're on the moon. There's rocks and dust and everything's horrible and you walk and then an idea like happens to you, an helicopter seed spins into your mind and roots push down into the soil –

Sam Dust?

Porsh It's soil now. Wet. Crumbly. And my feet sink into the moist earth.

Pause.

Sam Like in what?

Porsh Slow motion. Time lapse. White roots, black earth and a seed opens out into two like green . . .

Sam Leaves.

Porsh No, something else, the leaves come after and the flowers, but first – the seed.

Pause.

Sam I'm not talking about whatever it is you're talking about, I'm talkin' about Arnie. Lookin' in the mirror in this motel in the bathroom of this motel, man, and his face is a mess, all flesh gone and steel and mangle – so what's he do?

Porsh Flicks his hair.

Sam And don't you just *know* his cock is twelve inches of ice-cold steel.

Porsh pulls off her top – she's wearing bra and jeans.

Look . . . Don't stress me out, okay?

Porsh What you need is pain.

Sam Fuck off!

Porsh I'll show you.

Porsh finds a needle in her bag. She shows him the needle. Threads it up.

Sam What you doin'?

Porsh You need to feel the sharp. Pain and sex. Sharp and sharp. I understand.

Sam Yeah?

Porsh Don't be afraid.

Sam What you . . . Me? What you fuckin' talkin' . . . What you doin' with that?

Porsh This is the rod of ice-cold steel. This is the compass. And it points to you. Kiss kiss?

He looks at her with her top off, and kisses her. During the kiss she pushes the needle into his ear. He screams.

Sam Get it out!

Porsh You get it out.

Sam Get it out!

Porsh You get it out.

Sam Fuck off. My ear. My . . . My . . .

She pulls the needle through and ties off the cotton thread.

Porsh See.

Sam Careful. It hurts.

Porsh Moany.

Sam Too rough.

Porsh Enjoy.

Sam You what?

Porsh How is it? Better? You feel it spreading through you yet?

Pause.

Sam 'S all right.

Porsh I told you.

She feels his thigh.

Porsh Well?

Sam (*panicked*) Don't stress me. I don't. I can't. Just don't stress me out.

He stands up and ploughs his way through the videos. Then comes back. Pause.

Sorry about that. Rush.

Pause.

Porsh The films we soaked up in here. When I think of this place you know what I get: I get colour. Red and yellow and blue and pink so sweet your teeth buzz.

Sam Porsh . . .

Porsh The visual capacity of the human brain is equivalent to five hundred thousand television sets. That is a fact. I read it. Five hundred thousand. Skyscraper of screens.

Sam Porsh . . .

Porsh Skyscraper in the night. And we're lost inside all those windows.

Sam Speedin'.

Porsh I see . . . all my stories that I'm part of.

Sam SPEEDING!

Porsh Or all the stories that are part of me playin' on all the screens. Here.

Sam SLOW ME DOWN!

Porsh A silent rainbow ripples down in the corner – hundred screens, nothing. A wall of shiny, black glass except for . . . Nelson Eddy and Jeanette MacDonald: Naughty Marietta in the corner.

Sam Nelson Mandela?

Porsh Naughty Marietta!

Sam Mari . . . Mari . . .

Porsh *Etta*! You know, for that sad woman comes in for them films the owner only gets in 'cause he feels sorry for her.

Sam 'S better.

Porsh Otherwise the screens are full of glossy darkness. In which we wait.

Sam For what?

Porsh The sun. To carry on with our story. Everybody's got their story. What's yourn?

She unbuckles his belt.

Sam Private.

Porsh Who are you?

Sam Who are you?

Porsh shows him her breast – her nipple is pierced.

Porsh What d'you think?

He faces her.

Well?

Sam Can I touch it?

Porsh Go on.

Sam No, I can't . . .

Porsh Does it do it for you?

Sam Dunno.

Porsh Touch it.

He touches her nipple.

Sam Don't it hurt?

Porsh Try it and see.

Sam No way.

Porsh pulls up his shirt.

Porsh Do it and then you'll see.

Sam Keep that needle away from me.

Pause.

Sam Maybe I will.

Porsh Oh yeah?

Sam Tomorrow. At the parlour. They got pain-deadening sprays there.

Porsh Now.

Sam Tomorrow. Them pain deadening sprays are really good, you know?

Porsh Now.

Pause.

Sam Doesn't it hurt?

Porsh 'Course it fuckin' hurts. That's the point. I do yours. You do mine. And then we see.

Sam But you already got –

Porsh The other one. We do each other's.

Sam How about me other ear? I got two fuckin' ears, haven't I? Maybe it'll work with the next one.

Porsh holds another needle to his eyes. Sam turns his face away.
Bring up a light with Karen in it. She talks to Porsh.

Karen What happened then?

Sam Show me the needle.

Shows him a needle and thread. He looks.

How's this gonna help?

Porsh All depends on how you feel about pain.

Sam I feel bad about it, man.

Karen I feel bad about it too, man.

Sam's panic rises.

Sam Tell me about why again.

Porsh No.

She moves away.

You had your chance.

Sam Wait. I'm confused. Just tell me about why.

Porsh A person is a box with lots of different compartments but when something is lost from one of them, everything is wrong, there is a hole and you have to fill it up. That's where pain comes in.

Sam It works?

Porsh No question.

She unstraps his belt. Climbs astride him. They are face to face and breast to breast.

(*To Sam*) Now?

Sam In a minute.

Porsh Me you and you me.

Sam Give it here then.

Porsh One-two-three?

Sam One-two-three.

Porsh One-two-three then.

Sam One-two-three.

Karen Where'd you learn all this, Porsh?

Porsh (*to Karen, without looking*) Nowhere. I made it up. (*to Sam*) One . . . two . . .

Sam and Porsh THREE!

*They push the needles through each other's nipples. Blood and screams.
Blackout.*

SCENE THREE

In her light on the hospital park bench, Karen's radio blares. Porsh on. Karen is staring at her own breasts.

Karen Reckon my tits'll *ever* get back to normal?

Porsh No.

Karen Oh. I liked them little.

Porsh That is little.

Karen How *you* gonna manage the feeding? Babies can't work ring-pulls.

Porsh But I can. I'm gonna take them out so they work.

Karen Your lad worked –

Porsh Clockwork.

Porsh finds the spliff, and lights it.

Karen What colour baby you hoping for? I want reddy brown.

Porsh Karen, it doesn't necessarily work like that, this isn't Art.

Pause.

Karen I hated Art. Teacher got me suspended.

Porsh Let me guess –

Karen Just 'cos I stuck a modellin' knife in his hand. Served him right. Laughed at me drawin's. Cunt.

Pause.

My lad. Lad I met at 'ome up North. I'm his fluffybunny. He's a Paki. Met him in the kebaby.

Porsh Pakibunny.

Karen And dead romantic. Me wi' a weak 'eart and no Mum touched his romantic bone. So he asked me round his room for a romantic occasion.

Porsh Must really love you innit!

Karen All the trimmings. Dinner. Wine. Candles. Everything.

Porsh 'Cept Durex.

Karen It's against their religion.

Porsh Paki*man*! And what religion's that?

Karen Dunt know.

Porsh Sikh? Hindu? Moslem?

Karen Dunt rightly know about all that sort of thing.

Me Dad, he says: 'Fookin nigger.' – That's me Dad. - 'Norr havin' that black nigger norr in *my* house, norr in me fookin' daughter neither.' Slung me out, cunt, me Dad, temper on him. Any road, upshot were: me down here lookin for t'lad, 'cos he'd come down just before, reet? But he only fookin' disappears, dunt he? And it were only two days. And like all he said to guide me were: meet him under t'clock in fookin station.

Which fookin clock? Which fookin *station*?

Any road, I thought, it were only two days and he were bound to be waitin' in one of 'em, so I walked and it's this station, that station, one fookin' clock, t'other fookin' clock, station clock, clock station, station clock, till I don't know time of day or fookin' night. He's gone. He's gone, he's gone, he's gone, he's gone, he's gone.

Silence.

And he weren't black, he were brown. He weren't a nigger, he were a pak – *is* . . . is a pak . . .

Silence.

(*Sings*) Pak pak pak paki. Haven't had an egg since Christmas. And now it's half past three. Oh! . . .

Never quite rightly got straight about exactly what kind, but I trust him whatever he is. Wi' me life. 'Cos he's my lad he is. Wherever he is.

Pause.

Porsh *Thelma and Louise* is a film about these two women who ride off in this fuck-off smart car across the desert and get killed at the end.

Karen Is it a comedy?

Pause.

Porsh What you got?

Karen What?

Porsh In your bump?

Karen A girl. You?

Porsh Dunno.

Karen Dint they show you on the . . . ?

Porsh Ultrasound. I didn't look.

Karen You should have looked.

Porsh It might not be what I want.

Karen I looked. Fookin' *amazin'*! You know, Porsh, my little girl – my little girl is gonna mean the whole world to me. Can't help it, way I feel. More than the sun and stars.

Porsh I had a little girl once.

Karen More than chocolate.

Porsh They took her away.

Karen finally listens to Porsh.

Karen Your daughter?

Porsh My sister. You need . . . your own people round you. But I was too young to look after her. Not up to it.

Karen Gerrin' a bit lost here.

Porsh 'Look after your sister,' she goes. 'Promise me now,' and I do and she goes, 'All up to you, honey,' and then she goes – like, out.

Karen Your mother?

Porsh No right to that word.

Karen Because?

Porsh She died.

Karen Fookin' amazin' coincidence, man. So did *mine*.

Porsh turns up the radio.

Porsh But a promise is a promise.

Karen What?

Porsh A promise is a –

The Nurse rushes on and grabs the radio – Karen grabs the radio too. It's a stand-off. The Nurse pulls. Karen pulls back.

Karen Porsh.

Porsh walks threateningly towards the Nurse. Who lets go to maintain her dignity and steps back.

Nurse I'm going to . . .

Porsh Yes?

Nurse . . . confiscate that radio.

Porsh Unimpressive.

Nurse There are some very –

Porsh – very –

Karen – very –

Karen, Porsh *and* **Nurse** – ill people –

Nurse – in this hospital.

Karen turns the radio down. The Nurse goes. Stops.

Do I smell cigarettes? Have you been smoking?

Porsh and **Karen** No.

Nurse I hope not, because it's bad, very very bad for the baby.

The Nurse goes.

Karen Can't wait to get me hands on that soft little body. Love it to fookin' bits. Talc? Just you wait. Fookin' snowstorm!

Porsh puts her fingers in her mouth, sick-making.

I'm gonna watch her eyes all day long. I'm gonna swim in her eyes like she swims in me. Little brown eyes following me wherever I walk. A paintin'. And I'm gonna stop swearin'. And I got to walk.

She walks.

Karen Why do I always want a piss?

Porsh Baby's takin' all the space inside.

Karen Oh . . .

Porsh What?

Karen *Oh* . . .

Porsh What?

Karen *Oh* . . .

Porsh Fuckin' what? – *what*? – WHAT?

Karen Pins and needles.

Porsh Is that a sign?

Karen In me foot?

They look at her foot.

I don't think so.

Karen hops and shakes her foot.

Ridiculous fookin' state.

Porsh Karen.

Karen Yer what?

Porsh I'm wet.

Karen Where?

Porsh Between me legs. What's wet mean?

Karen You need the toilet.

Porsh No, it's startin'.

Karen stands.

Karen (*top of lungs*) HELP!

Karen walks.

Karen HELP!

Porsh Don't get frightened.

Karen I'm not.

Porsh I know you are, but don't. It'll be all right. I'll be here. Just don't leave me.

Karen, terrified, could run at any moment. But decides to stay.

Karen Reet.

Porsh Promise.

Karen I promise.

Porsh And I won't leave you.

Karen Promise?

Porsh Promise.

Karen And you won't die?

Porsh No. I promise.

She grabs Porsh's hand.

Karen HELP!

Porsh Don't leave me.

Karen I won't.

Porsh Don't let go.

Karen I won't. What do I do?

Porsh Hold me.

They hang on to each other.

Karen Oh God.

Porsh What?

Karen I'm wet.

Blackout.

SCENE FOUR

Hospital delivery room. Musak. But terrible sounds of labour are coming from Karen in the delivery room next door.
  Porsh, giving birth, in the nightie and the boots, is spread – with Tommy between her open legs.

Tommy Nearly there. Okay. Shit. Right. Right. The monitor's on the baby's scalp.

Porsh Oh! So that's why your face was up me crack?

He stops, distracted – looks at her face.

Don't stop!

Tommy Sorry.

Porsh New at this, incha?

Karen (*shouts*) Porsh!

Porsh (*shouts*) Karen!

Karen (*off*) Por.

Porsh (*shouts*) Kar!

Karen (*off*) Help me. Help me. Oh no. Oh no. Oh no.

Porsh Hang on Kar.

Karen (*off*) Help me. Help me.

Porsh It'll be all right.

Tommy picks up a rule and measures the cervical dilation.

Where'd you leave the rest of your geometry kit then?

Tommy I'm measuring cervical dilation. Eight centimetres.

Porsh Never mind, you can get it extended.

Tommy We're not far off now.

Porsh We?

Tommy Another two centimetres.

Porsh I bet – I bet you – you was one of them kids never lost your rubber I was always lending off of at school. Lend us your rubber, lend us –

Porsh is overtaken by a contraction.

– lend us – Needle! Kar!

Karen (*off*) Por!

The Nurse comes on.

Nurse Doctor. In here.

He walks to look at the door into Karen's labour ward – from where we hear her grunting.

Porsh Needle!

Tommy Under the circumstances, pentathol wouldn't be a very good idea.

Porsh Fuck you, give it me.

Tommy Maybe an epidural.

Karen (*off*) Mam. Where are you? Mam.

Nurse It's okay, honey, I'm coming.

She goes.

Tommy I've bleeped the anaesthetist. But she's not here yet. There must be an emergency.

Porsh Give it me that needle NOW!

Tommy And it does say on your notes – somewhere – that you don't want – I think I saw . . .

Tommy reads the notes.

Porsh Give it. Give it me!

Tommy That you didn't want –

Porsh Now! Now! Now! Aaaaaaaaaaaaaaah!!

Tommy Hold on.

Porsh Aaaaaaaaaaaaaaah!!

Karen (*off*) Aaaaaaaaaaaaaaah!!

Tommy Hold on.

He runs out.

(*Off*) Hold on.

Porsh pants through the contraction. Karen makes sounds of distress.

Hold on.

He runs off.

Porsh Who to?

Tommy runs on.

Tommy Me.

Porsh You are useless.

He examines her.

Tommy Shit. It's coming too fast, you've got to hold back.

Porsh You have done this before?

Tommy Of course.

Porsh Needle.

Tommy Where's that fucking anaesthetist?

Porsh Gas then. Gimme gas.

Tommy applies gas and air. Porsh takes it, then gradually comes out of her contraction. Leans back.

Shit music. Here. Put this on.

She hands him a tape.

Tommy I'm not supposed to change the music. The nurses do that. They get really annoyed if you interfere.

Porsh How many times you done this?

Tommy Lots of times.

Porsh Liar.

Tommy Honestly.

Porsh Liar.

Tommy This is my – my second.

Porsh Second? No way. Nobody begins with their first. This is your first.

Pause.

Tommy Okay, but I've seen lots.

Porsh *Seen*!

Tommy As a student.

Porsh *Student*! Oh fuck, no.

Tommy And the midwife is just –

Porsh Where?

Tommy Next door. So there's no problem whatsoever.

From the next delivery room comes a blood-curdling scream.

Porsh I've changed me mind. I'm too young. And so are you! Why do I always get practised on by middle-class wankers? I want a real doctor, not some boy.

Tommy It's the middle of the night, and I'm the best doctor there is right now.

Porsh sits on the floor as another contraction overtakes her. She shouts.

Porsh Aaaaaagh!

Tommy Breathe.

Porsh Cunts.

Tommy Breath, it helps the pain.

Porsh Fuckin' cunts.

Tommy Hold onto me.

She clings to him.

That's better.

Porsh Oh my God, I hate all of you people.

Tommy Tell me something.

Porsh Nice eyes, green. Nice teeth. Nice lashes. Long. Milky white boy.

Tommy Something about yourself. Anything.

Pause.

Porsh I'm fourteen.

Tommy Oh. It says eighteen in your file.

Porsh This is a story. I'm fourteen and in the children's home and my boots are so – Gas! Gas, gas!

He gets it, she fills her lungs. Porsh takes the mask off.

DMs don't come with more holes. I'm laced halfway up to my arse in these hard boots. And patois is expected. So hard! So what? 'Cos they always gotcha, innit? Why? 'Cos you lost your baby sister to some shopkeeper and you can't ever get her back.

Tommy Where is she?

Porsh Manchester. Fostered.

Tommy Don't you see her?

Porsh Can't. Face. Gas.

She takes the gas.

(*Into mask*) Aaaaaaaaaaaaaaaaaaaaah!

Talks to him between the gas.

Porsh C'mon, give me that needle!

Tommy No. *I can't. I'm not – it's hospital policy that –*

Porsh Noooooooooooooooo!

Tommy Hold back or you'll tear.

Porsh Get me that woman.

Tommy Hold back or I'll have to stitch you and neither of us want that.

Porsh Get that woman then!

Off – the sounds of Karen's birth rise towards a crescendo.

Tommy She's fully occupied.

Porsh Then give me the needle!

The contraction stops and she relaxes for a minute.

Tommy What was that one like?

Porsh Shitting basketballs.

Tommy Why can't you face your sister?

Porsh Because I haven't put everything right yet. Do me a favour and take out me rings. And remember you're a doctor.

He takes out her nipple rings.

Enjoy that?

Abruptly, another contraction.

FUCK!

Nurse on.

Nurse Do you want your child to come into the world to the sound of obscenity?

Porsh Obscenity is a freedom I take – allow – assume, on account of my extensive vocabulary. Arsehole to zombie. Allow myself the luxury of abusing silly middle-class people what live off my back.

Nurse Look at those boots! Come here, with those boots –

Porsh Touch them boots and this baby come in your mouth. Make a change something come in your mouth.

Nurse Where you get to talk so Caribbean in Lewisham, child?

Porsh You – oooooooooooooooow!

Nurse Serve you right.

The noise reaches a crescendo from next door.

Karen (*off*) Porsh!

Porsh Karen!

Karen (*off*) Don't leave me.

Porsh I won't leave you.

Nurse goes. Tommy bends in. Porsh falls back exhausted.

Gimme the needle, man.

Tommy No.

Porsh A fag then. I can tell you smoke from the smell.

Tommy I couldn't

Porsh I won't grass.

Tommy It's not fair on the baby.

Porsh You're an intelligent boy – you know there's a certain amount of propaganda. I don't inhale. One fag – come on! You then, and let me smell it.

He lights up. She smells. Swoons.

Porsh Your fault. You should have insisted I didn't. No control. Too weak. Nice eyes though. Deep. How many A-levels?

Tommy Four.

Porsh That's not fair.

Tommy I'm sorry.

Porsh Actually, I got five GCSEs, including Maths and English.

Tommy That's good.

Porsh Don't patronise me.

Tommy You patronise me.

Porsh I lied. All I've got's my plan.

The screams from next door are very bad. The Nurse bursts in. Tommy hides the cigarette.

Nurse Doctor!

Tommy Right.

Nurse What's that smell? Cigarettes!?

Tommy What are you suggesting, nurse?

The Nurse goes. Porsh throws him a tape.

Porsh Tape. Gonna put me boots on, get her out of here.

Tommy I have to go.

Porsh So go. Music.

Tommy turns on the tape. Very loud drumbeat music.

Tommy I'll be back.

Porsh 'S okay, I'm strong. I'm special.

*Tommy dashes.
Porsh on her own.*

Porsh Oh God. It's coming. Please, God, not a boy. A boy's no use. MUMMY!

Fade down on Porsh as her Mother (played by the same actress who played the Nurse) walks on with two bare chairs. Arranges them facing each other.

Mother You always was a noisy girl. You ever stop with making your noise, huh? Ruth? I'm talking now, Ruth.

Porsh Why Ruth?

Her Mother opens the Bible.

Mother Because she is right there in my Bible, honey. Ruth. Knee-deep in the alien corn.

Porsh No corn grow in Lewisham, Mum.

Mother (*smiles*) But corn in Jamaica, honey. Banana. Cane right up to your eyes. An' mango just droppin' down into your hand. You put out your hand and the fruit drop right into it. Like that. And papaya piled up just like on Dalston Market. Only cheaper.

Porsh Yeah yeah yeah – so what about the Ruth?

Mother (*giving her the Bible*) You find her. She's in there. I found her there for you, darlin'. You look now.

Porsh finds the place. The Mother talks from memory.

(*Reads*) In the time of the Judges. All has been told. How you left your father and your mother. Came to Bethlehem at the harvest. Came to a people you did not know. Ruth.

Porsh Leave me alone now, Mum. It hurts.

Mother You called me, honey.

Porsh But I didn't mean it. My defences was down.

Mother You called me and you know I want to hear. What did you do with my baby?

Porsh I'm the one having the baby.

Mother Then you got something for me, I think.

Porsh The baby is mine.

Mother How can that be, honey? All the little babies is mine because you lost my little baby.

Porsh You said you'd come back and you lied. You just left.

Mother Well, where I am we call that dying. And you not rememberin' straight, girl, what I *left* was you in charge, what I *left* you with was something to take care of. You taken care of that little thing I left you?

Porsh I tried.

Tommy comes on and they deliver the baby.

Mother You taken care a' her?

Porsh Too hard.

Mother Why?

Porsh Too young.

Mother Just not good enough! I'm takin' this one to fill her place.

Mother walks away. Stops.

So you let her out, right now. My little girl.

Tommy It's a boy.

Pause.

Mother Ruth. You nothin' but a disappointment to me all your life, you know that?

Blackout.

SCENE FIVE

Porsh in bed, turned to the wall. Tommy in his doctor's coat.

Tommy Can I sit down?

Pause.

The nurses say you won't look at your baby.

Porsh So?

Tommy I don't understand.

Porsh Why didn't you give me the needle when I asked? Fuckin' thing eatin' it's way out. I was yellin' my 'ead off and you didn't take no notice.

Tommy I couldn't.

Porsh You was givin' me pain, man.

Tommy No. Everything happened very fast, there was no time.

Porsh Tell the truth!

Tommy And I was frightened.

Porsh And you cut me.

Tommy Afraid so. There were two of you at once. I had to act.

Porsh And you couldn't wait for somebody qualified, could ya? 'Cos it's only slag and don't matter.

Tommy You'd have torn and that would have been worse.

Porsh I don't tear, I'm not paper!

Tommy And I am qualified. I did my best. Actually, I did rather well.

Porsh You cut me in two.

She looks at him. He takes her in his arms. She cries. He lets her go.

Tommy He is very beautiful.

Porsh That is a shit link.

Tommy Like you.

Pause.

I didn't mean to say that.

Porsh Say it again.

Tommy You're my patient. I have a role. I have professional responsibilities.

Porsh Innit.

She turns away.

Tommy You didn't want him?

Porsh I wanted *her*!

Tommy Boy – girl – does it matter so much?

Porsh I have a plan.

Tommy A girl to take your sister's place?

Porsh Oh . . . Oh . . . He finally read my file, and now he knows all about me.

Tommy I know that when your mother died, you looked after your sister.

Porsh Tried. Failed. 'You know what I mean.'

Tommy Jesus Christ, give yourself a break, you were only nine. And you managed for three months on your own in that flat. How did you do it?

Porsh (*sarcastic*) I'm special.

Pause.

Tommy What are her foster parents like?

Porsh Dunno.

Tommy And you don't see her?

Porsh No. I'm no use. No use to her.

Tommy Because you think you let her down?

Porsh Don't touch me!

Tommy I'm just telling you what I think.

Porsh White boy.

Tommy I'm not a boy; I'm a doctor.

Porsh And you look at my file and you know exactly who I am, doctor: reports, histories, assessments, explanation. Get off my back. Because I am not that cliché. That is not who I am. Somebody else.

Tommy Yeah, but –

Porsh I have a plan.

Tommy You also have a son.

She grabs the cigarettes from his white coat pocket. Lights up.

Porsh My social worker cracked up last week.

Tommy Yeah?

Porsh Walked past the office and saw him through the door. You know what he was doing? He goes: 'Aaaaah.' (*Acts crying.*) Cryin'! On – my – time! What the fuck these people think they for anyway?

Tommy It's a very demanding job.

Porsh It's a very demanding life, White Boy. I am his client and I demand respect. I am your patient and where is my clean shirt?

She flicks his collar. He reacts to the touch.

Hey . . .

Pause. Tommy breaks away from the look.

The way you white boys go red, man. No.

Tommy Excuse me?

Porsh No. Thirty-six hours is a bit soon to test your stitchin'.

Tommy I came to say that he needs you.

Porsh He's got to learn people who need suffer. Don't you know that? So young.

Tommy Older than you.

Porsh Only in years.

She grabs Tommy's hands. He tries but can't let go.

Why so embarrassed, after where these have been? Oh, they've led an easy life these hands. No hard edges here.

Tommy Need to be soft where they go.

Porsh And not quite as clever as they think they are.

Tommy They delivered two babies last night.

She puts the hands on her face.

Porsh Say what I am again. The word.

Tommy Beautiful.

Porsh Beautiful.

Pause.

Porsh Uh-huh! I'm hippy. I got a big nose. Me ankles is tree trunks and I swear all the time.

Tommy In your own way.

Porsh In my own way! What you will tell me now is that everybody is, like, *so* beautiful in their own way.

Tommy In your own way.

Porsh What way's that then?

Tommy I think we've strayed out of the professional . . . professional . . .

Porsh Orbit.

Tommy Orbit.

Porsh Don't talk, touch.

He slides his hands down her arms.

Tommy I'm your doctor . . .

Porsh Don't lie. Your dick is glowin' like skiplight. Name?

Tommy Doctor –

Porsh Your *real* name.

Tommy Thomas.

Porsh What d'you get?

Tommy Tommy.

Porsh Tommy Cool Hands.

Tommy Did you touch him?

She pulls away and back to the wall.

Porsh My eyes were closed.

Tommy You fed him.

Porsh I was being fair – giving him the . . .

Tommy Colestrum.

Porsh I know, I fucking *know*!

Tommy You won't even look at him.

Porsh If I look at him, just once, I'm lost.

Tommy God has a plan for everybody, and for your son – you are it.

Porsh Easy for you to say. It's me that has to live it. On me own.

She faces the wall. He touches her. She grabs his hand.

Don't let go.

Tommy No.

Porsh Promise.

Tommy I promise. I won't let go.

Porsh You have to mean it . . .

Tommy I mean it Ruth.

Porsh I get Porsh.

Tommy Why?

Porsh Don't matter.

Tommy Portia?

Pause.

The quality of mercy is not strained. Shakespeare.

Porsh I know.

Tommy sits back, about to go.

Wait. Teach me?

Pause.

Tommy If you like.

Pause.

Porsh Show me.

Tommy lifts the baby from the cot. And shows him to Porsh. She turns. The lights dim. She cries out – softly. Blackout.

SCENE SIX

Porsh's flat. A secondhand cot. A buggy. And a bath. A door. Sam, desperate, leans on the other side of the door.

Porsh, in bedclothes, is lighting birthday candles. And sticking them in plasticine on the edge of the cot. Her application form is on the floor beside her.

Karen sitting in a bath wearing a huge T-shirt and nothing else, clutching her radio to her weak heart. On the floor, a kettle is heating up.

Karen Your own place?

Porsh Yeah.

Karen So, what you got against furniture?

Porsh It costs money.

Karen Candles and no chairs? What's all them candles for, then, like?

Porsh lights another candle.

I like them.

Karen Oh. Fair enough, then.

Porsh His eyes follow the flame.

Karen Murder a cup of tea.

Porsh moves the candle over the cot. Karen turns away from the cot.

Is that a banana over there?

Porsh See that light in his eyes? That's light dancing in the deep well of his soul, man. Fantastic.

Karen I love – I love – I love . . . banana. Bananarama.

D'you know how many calories there are in a banana? Kettle's boiling. Kettle. It's boilin'. Look.

Porsh spills candle wax onto her application form. Tries to wipe it off.

Porsh Oh no.

Karen (*wild reaction*) What? What?

Porsh Me application form.

Karen For what?

Porsh Just look at it.

Tries to clean it. As Karen focuses on the kettle.

Porsh Mess.

Karen Murder, fookin' murder a cup of fookin' tea. Me mouth's all dry.

Porsh makes tea. Karen turns and stares unblinking at the baby.

Sweet. Gorr any cake?

Porsh No cake.

Karen Coffee?

Porsh Just tea.

Porsh pours tea.

Karen Tea's great. Me mind's so like – wi' names and that . . . ?

Porsh Porsh.

Karen But you get Ruth.

Porsh No, Ruth but I get Porsh.

Karen Helicopter.

Porsh Right. Some first word, helicopter, man, innit? Polysyllabic.

Karen takes the mug.

Karen Gorrany sugar?

Porsh I don't, it's bad.

Karen *Sugar?*

Porsh Rots your teeth and makes you fat.

Karen It's all reet in moderation. I like milk in my tea. Have you – ?

Porsh Just powder.

Karen Okay. That'll do.

Porsh No.

Karen I don't mind.

Porsh Look, all I've got's tea. Like this.

They drink. Karen can't manage it.

Karen Something up wi' me throat. Sore! Am I achin' everywhere or what!? (*Washes.*) This fookin' water. Look arrit! There's bits in it. Like soup.
   Oooo *God*! Tharr *'urts*. I'm that sore. I've been *well* fooked.

Porsh Who by?

Karen Dunno. Not exactly. But just the one, I think but . . . hey, but I were out of me brain, apparently.

Porsh With what?

Karen Dunt matter.

Porsh What happened?

Karen Can't remember! So dint happen, worrever it was. All gone, dunt matter, in control.

She turns on her radio.

Do this?

Karen tries the handjive, badly. Porsh grabs the radio.

Porsh Like fuck. So there I am walkin' through the hospital car park and there you are. Like this.

Sarcastically, Porsh clutches the radio and does a slow, stoned, stumble-dance.

Dancin' in the street, like –

Karen Great.

Porsh In control.

Karen 'Tastic.

Porsh My arse. (*Abruptly snaps radio off and stops dancing.*) And what you doin' back at the hospital, Karen?

Karen Big place that hospital.

Karen reaches for the radio. Porsh keeps it out of her reach.

Porsh Where is she?

Silence. Karen is stopped dead. Porsh folds the girl to herself. Disengages.

Thinner, Kar. Thought that was impossible.

Karen Where's me clothes?

Porsh I chucked them. Stinkin' the place out.

Karen But they were me *clothes*!

Porsh No, it was just you wearing them they was somebody else's and I was not having them dirty horrible rags in my flat. Get clean, Karen. Do you hear me?

Karen (*shouts*) Give me some soap then?

Porsh gives her soap. Walks. Karen lunges, grabs her arm.

Dunt leave me. I didn't mean it.

Porsh I'm walking across the room! I'm getting you some clothes.

Karen Stay where I can see you. I'm not takin' a chance on you not come back wi' me clothes and me left bare arse in fookin' water fook knows where.

Porsh walks, Karen lunges out of the water and follows her. Porsh wraps her in the white coat she has picked up.

Dunt leave me, Helicopter.

Porsh Chicken.

Karen Promise, Helicopter.

Porsh I promise. How you feelin'?

Karen Fine

Pause.

Porsh I'm startin' him on the bottle tomorrow.

Karen stares at the baby again.

Porsh I'm quite nervous, actually. He's used to me, in he? Don't think it's too much for one day – do ya? – I mean that and everything else. What d' you think?

Pause. Then as if nothing had happened.

Karen Breast's best. Wunt win wet teeshirt contest but I know what's what.

Karen stares ostentatiously at the remaining banana.

I'm still hungry. Do you know how many calories there are in a –

Pushes the banana into her hand.

Porsh Every woman in The Western World is born knowin' how many calories in a banana. DRINK!

Kelly drinks.

Is Kelly on the bottle?

Silence.

'Cos you obviously int feedin' her, are you?

Karen reaches for the radio, but Porsh throws it aside.

Porsh I haven't got time for this. I've got my giro to cash, then I'm goin'. And you comin' with me. Get dressed.

Porsh throws Karen some trousers and a pullover. Karen picks them up.

Karen All eyes, int yer?

Porsh Shy?

Karen Fookin likely!

Nevertheless, Karen turns her back and dresses modestly.

Porsh Tommy'll be here any minute.

Karen Who?

Porsh Boy. Special boy. The doctor who delivered my baby – and your baby – don't you remember him?

Karen No.

Porsh Soft hands. Makes me feel so . . . Come round to see me afterwards.

Karen Didn't come to see me.

Porsh He's always late. Just have to miss me this time, won't he.

The baby grizzles. Porsh has the form in one hand as she digs down inside the nappy to check its state.

Shit. Fuck. Made a mistake. Fed him too early. An hour ago. Just an hour? His nappy'll be full of horrible smelly stuff. I mean, we're goin' out, I don't want to get into that, not this mornin'. Should have thought of that. Oh no!

Porsh has messed the form again, this time with baby shit. She tries to clean it up.

Have to do.

Karen You can't resist a baby's cry.

Porsh I thought you were supposed to have gone back up north.

Karen I did.

Porsh Kelly?

Karen reaches for the radio, Porsh intercepts yet again.

Karen Give her to Mam.

Porsh Don't lie. You told me your mother is dead.

Karen I meant his Mam, me Paki-lad's Mam back home, I left her wi' them 'cos they know more about that kind of thing, them lot. Did I tell you I'm meetin' him underneath clock in t'station, me Paki-lad? He's in the building trade. Brilliant wi' roofs is my lad. Him and his brother can strip, felt and retile in a day and all for seven hundred quid. They dunt use scaffolds you see. Dependin' on size of roof of course. He were workin' on a roof when I met him. Him an' his brother. On the roof next door to me

Dad's house. Me Dad were at work and I wunt at school so I stood in the garden and looked up an' there he were in the sun, all brown and shiny.

Pause.

We're gonna get our own house. Eventually. And he's gonna renovate it up. Dunt laugh at me!

Porsh I'm not.

Karen Dunt lie.

Porsh jumps to her feet.

Porsh NO!

Karen Fook!

Porsh He's here.

Karen Special boy?

Porsh Sam.

The door is kicked.

Karen (*wild*) Sam who? Where? What the fook?

Porsh Go away.

Karen Me heart.

Porsh Leave me alone!

Sam (*off*) Let me in.

Porsh Leave us alone!

Sam (*off*) Please let me in.

Karen Dunt.

Porsh You int comin' in!

Sam (*off*) Open this door or I kick it in.

Porsh I'm never gonna let you in!

Sam (*off*) You know I'll do it.

Porsh Try and die.

Sam (*off*) I'm gonna.

Porsh And you dead.

The kicking stops. Sam starts crying on the other side of the door. Porsh leans against it.

Sam (*off*) He's mine too.

Porsh Don't shout. Don't cry. You'll wake the baby. Shush. Hush, Sammy. Hush now or you'll wake Peter.

Sam (*off*) Let me see him.

Porsh Shush.

Sam (*off*) I need to see him.

Porsh (*to the door*) He'll start cryin'.

Sam (*off*) Things'll be different.

Porsh You'll wake him.

Karen He's awake.

Sam (*off*) Who's that in there with you?

Porsh My friend.

Sam (*off*) You don't know what you are doing to me, you don't know how I feel. I am warning you! Porsh? What kind of friend?

Porsh Karen.

Sam Listen. Listen. I can't handle this because, like, listen . . . your judgement, it goes, man and you feel so desperate, and it builds up and up, you fight it, you try and try but it builds up in you and deep down, all of us, we're only human. I will not give in!

Porsh Neither will I.

Sam I'll be back. And back. And back.

Sam goes. They wait. Pause.

Porsh He's gone.

Porsh moves away from the door.

Karen What was that?

Porsh The past.

Karen Can I stay? I mean come. Just till I meet me lad and get meself sorted out an' that. I'm great now and I'll keep out the way when your lad's round. Come on.

Karen moves.

Porsh No!

Karen What?

Porsh Wait.

Karen I gorra weak heart in here y'know. Why?

Porsh He might be waiting. Give it a minute. And get that paper.

Karen picks up the application form.

Karen Ugh!

Passes it to Porsh who irons it with her hand on the floor and puts it in her bag.

Porsh Have to do.

They wait. Porsh opens the door, looks.

Karen Hey, remember *Thelma and Louise*?

Porsh 'No. Which ward they in then?'

Karen Dunt get you?

Porsh Never will neither. Go!

Blackout.

SCENE SEVEN

Porsh's flat.
Sofa. Cot. Tommy sits on the floor staring into space. He is deeply troubled. The doorbell! He opens the door. Sam pushes in. Tommy backs away. They stare.

Tommy For Ruth?

Sam drops his heavy sports bag.

Yeah. Ruth isn't here right now –

Sam She gets Porsh.

Tommy I know.

Sam Why didn't you say it then?

Tommy Because . . .

Sam Yeah?

Tommy Because I didn't know you knew.

Sam Why wouldn't you think I'd know that?

Tommy Because I don't know who you are.

Sam No?

Tommy No. And I don't know why you're here.

Pause.

Sam *Sam*. And I'm here because that's who I am. Sam the man.

Tommy No offence, right, but I've just come round and I want –

Sam Come round? Come – and no *offence*?

Tommy Whatever. She isn't here. (*Looks round.*) Apparently.

Sam And you are, Mr. Apparently. Mr. Whothefuck.

Tommy turns on him and Sam backs quickly away. Tommy controls himself.

Tommy A friend of Porsh's? Right, you've probably had some kind of hard time but so have I. This could be the worst day of my life.

Sam Tell me.

Tommy You couldn't –

Sam Too thick.

Tommy Have you held a baby in your hands, brand new, seconds old?

Silence.

Sam Not seconds. Hours. Days. But not –

Tommy In your hands. And then some stupid little cunt . . .

Sam Some fucking cunt!

Tommy Who are you?

Sam Sam the Spam.

Tommy Well, Sam the Spam, I got a couple of videos and I need a little *lightness*, a little pleasure, so if you don't mind fucking off at least till –

Sam Films? (*Picks up the videos.*) Subway? That's not a film, that's an 'ole in the ground.

Tommy Hey. Porsh will, I am sure, be delighted to entertain an old friend as charming as yourself, when she comes back!

Sam Don't you even want to know what I want to talk to her about? You don't even know what I want to *say*?

Tommy No.

Sam I want . . . to like speak my mind – laugh, go on – His mind. His fuckin' mind. That won't take long will it?

Tommy I hope not.

Sam People . . .

Tommy (*sings Streisand*) 'Who need people.'

Sam I don't get you.

Tommy (*sings*) 'Are the luckiest people in the world.'

Sam People like you, you twist things.

Tommy No, to be fair, I don't think so. What actually happened here is you barged in here –

Sam Barged!

Tommy *Barged.*

Sam Twistin'! Bargin'!

Tommy (*quietly*) And sticking one on you any second now.

Sam I'M NOT SHIT!

Pause.

Tommy Well. Now that's settled, just go. Fuck Subway. Fuck Helena Bonham Carter. I just want sleep.

Sam You sleep here?

Tommy Any second.

Sam Fuck here as well? Fuck on the sofa? On the floor? Spread out a really expensive rug and wrap up in it. Her legs round your waist pullin' you in.

Pause.

Tommy Oh shit. It's . . . Listen, I didn't realise –

Sam *No.* You don't. Till it's too late.

Sam walks into the room.

You close your eyes and you're back in the actual moment. Before. When everything is in order. And then it's afterwards when everything is in pieces and you don't get it but you don't care because all you want is to go back. (*points*) This place! Here. This is where it happened. The same spot. Breathe this air. Same air, man.

I come in. Stand in the doorway. There. Look round at the flat – Oh yes! Nice one! – Walk in and I go: spacious! (*Walks into the space.*) And I go: things can happen here. Then she looks and goes: no. So I look and go: what? She turns away her head, like this, and goes: no. I go: what? She goes: not for you. I go: me? Yes, she goes: you. I go: don't get you? And she goes: I know and you never will.

Pause.

Never will. At first the words don't take. But then when they do your head floats right off, man. I go, I go: W-w-w-w-w-w-, spluttering like a cunt, w-w-why not? She goes: 'cos you're out. What? – Out. – The push. – The what? – Me? – You. – WHY? – Just accept it.

Pause.

ACCEPT IT? JUST ACCEPT IT?

Pause.

WELL, IT INT JUST HER IS IT!? There's the little kiddie to think of and he's got to have his Dad. Do you think I like ruinin' people's lives?

Tommy No.

Sam No. 'Course not. None of this would have happened if my Dad had been around. That's why I am so useless. Well, no, it int happenin' to Peter. I will be here!

What I say is it's not nice not to have a Dad all his life and I'm ready, I'm waiting, but, no, because actually I'm out, little Petey's Dad is out. And you are in. Well in, incha?

Pause.

Tommy It's a shitty day all round.

Sam I reckon the baby put something into her brain about me. Baby hormones fuckin' up her brain ' cos women get odd. Oddness. And, you know, this int fair 'cos my intentions are like NEVER BEFORE . . . To make a life for my kiddie! Why can't she just *LISTEN TO ME*?

Tommy turns away. Sam takes a baseball bat out of the sports bag.

She will. When the hormones is off the scene. And you.

Tommy Me?

Sam You.

Tommy turns as Sam spins with the baseball bat. Hits Tommy. Tommy falls.

When you off the scene.

Tommy stunned, on the floor, almost unconscious. Sam sits and looks at him.

You think I'm just an ignorant cunt. No, don't lie. Well you're wrong. I know all kinds of things.

Pause.

Take wolves f'r instance. (*growls*) They have this way of sleeping for just a few minutes and then wake themselves right up. Like this. (*spins*) People got wolves wrong.

Think they're just big lollopin' dogs round the prairie, like fuckin' big dogs, man. No, no, no – wrong! Organisation is the key to success. The pack. The alpha male at the top. The only and unquestioned leader. And the only one allowed to mate, which, by the way, is right out of the picture for you, from now on.

Sam produces his knife and Tommy jerks away.

Wait!

Tommy waits.

Mr Wolf-My-Man picks out the prey from the herd. Goes: that one. And then they run down that prey. Mile after mile and never give in 'cos they know they gonna win. And then when the deer or whatever crashes down, done in, Mr Wolf-My-Man goes: wait! Stroll over. Look down at the – love this word – the *prey* and take a moment.

Pause.

There's a big, fat pulse in your neck. Just there.

Pause.

I can do anything I want with you.

Pause.

Love hurts.

Pause.

My Mum was always too soft with me, and look what happens? No, no way I'm lettin' him go without a Dad. Droppin' kids all over the place with lots of different ladies and no Dad, that's not nice. But *Porsh*, she is so special, and she says: *no*! And no argument, 'cos all of a sudden it int mine. Whose is it then? Yours?

Tommy shakes his head.

'Course not.

Tommy gasps and sobs.

Sam Where is she?

Tommy I don't know.

Sam 'COURSE YOU DO!

Tommy I don't.

Sam Don't you give me that.

Tommy Sainsburys.

Sam Don't you give me Sainsburys.

Tommy The clinic, maybe the –

Sam Don't you give me the clinic.

Tommy College then.

Sam What?

Tommy It's a guess.

Sam Why?

Tommy She wants to get on a course.

Sam What for?

Tommy A-level English. I told her they won't take her.

Sam Where's your dignity?

Tommy stops sobbing.

College? I didn't know about that.

Tommy Hey . . . she could be anywhere.

Sam Grass.

Tommy Lots of places.

Sam So where's she find a piece of shit like you, then?

Tommy She might be at the hospital.

Sam Why?

Tommy I'm a doctor.

Sam But you're here. Where's she then?

Tommy The hospital.

Sam (*panic*) Petey's at the hospital?

Tommy He's fine.

Sam What she go to the hospital for then?

Tommy Check-ups.

Sam How'd you know?

Tommy That's where we met.

Sam Oh. I'm going to get you struck off, mate.

Pause.

So you come in and take everything over. What about the rightful father? You thought I wouldn't care.

Tommy I didn't know.

Pause.

Sam They know how to do things in films, though.

Pause.

Tommy That's true.

Sam Some people call them videos, I call them films.

Tommy So do I.

Sam What?

Tommy I don't know. Whatever it is we're talking about.

Sam formally walks five paces.

Sam You there. Me there.

Tommy Is this a film?

Sam There's mist, and there's grass. We're on the edge of the forest and our breath is cold, white smoke in the air. Winter. And silence. Except maybe for just one bird. Then they open the –

Tommy Who – ?

Sam I'll lose the thread! – Then they open the case and show us the pistols in their blood-red velvet box. Hexagonal barrels. Blue steel.

Sam taps Tommy's head with the baseball bat.

Tommy You've got me wrong.

Sam And you look up at the old man under the branches. *He* is the doctor.

Tommy Believe me.

Sam *Him*, not you. But he don't save you 'cause the bullet is already in your heart. In your dead fuckin' heart you fuckin' cunt.

Pause.

Porsh talk about me?

Tommy Yes.

Sam What did she say?

Tommy She said that she worked in a video shop once with this . . . boy.

Sam This ' . . . ' boy. This ' . . . ' 'bad' boy. This ' . . . ' 'thick' boy. This 'limpdick' boy. Well she's a liar! She never worked there. *I* worked there and she is a liar.

Tommy Okay.

Sam Everybody has a story. And if you're lucky you play it right but if you're not, the tape gets mangled up. My story is all mashed up with her –

Sam opens the bag – it is a shitty nappy. He gags.

Oh . . . oh . . . disgustin' –

He retches.

Disgustin'.

He recovers.

I was just a prawn in her plan.

Tommy A prawn in her pilau.

Sam I wasn't lucky like you, sleep on her pillow, all I was to her was just a spunk bubble. Peter was no accident. That's okay. But then she wanted him all to herself. I mean: gutted, or what? Well . . .

Sam begins packing.

College.

Tommy Clinic.

Sam College.

As Sam tapes up Tommy's mouth.

Tommy Park . . .

Sam College.

Sam experimentally taps Tommy's head with the bat.

Sam I want to kill you so much. But Petey wouldn't like it when he grows up.

Tommy Now I think about it, she did mention Sainsbury's.

Tommy all taped up.

Sam Fear speaks true.

Blackout.

SCENE EIGHT

Further Education College – classroom. Sonia at a desk – looks up as Karen and Porsh rush in. They have Sainsbury's carrier bags. Karen stops at the door looking out.

Porsh I saw him.

Karen Did he see you?

Porsh Dunno.

Karen Who? Who? Who we talkin' about?

Porsh The one who kicked the door of the flat.

Karen You saw him for definite?

Porsh For definite

Karen Oh fook. What's he going to do?

Porsh Hard to say.

Karen Oh fook. He see us or not?

Porsh Dunno. But I'm not takin' the chance.

Karen Is he bad?

Porsh Big question. Bad? Yeah. But not in the good way.

Karen Is he fookin' dangerous?

Porsh Oh yeah.

Karen looks into the corridor.

Karen What's he look like?

Porsh Rat. Hunched up. Pointy ears.

Karen There's nobody like that.

Porsh Stay there.

Karen Reet.

Sonia Excuse me.

Porsh Yeah –

Karen Listen out though, listen for me in case I call.

Porsh I do. (*to Sonia*) Hello.

Sonia Hello.

Porsh Hello.

Sonia Your friend – what does she mean, listen? For whom?

Porsh Ask me.

Sonia Well, I thought I just did.

Porsh No. Anything.

Sonia takes in the buggy, Porsh's desperation.

Sonia Your baby?

Porsh He's okay.

Sonia It shouldn't be in the teaching area.

Porsh He.

Sonia There are regulations.

Karen No sign.

Porsh Right.

Karen Worr 'appens if a crowd comes down?

Porsh They won't, it's holidays.

Karen But what if they do?

Porsh They won't.

Karen But what if they DO?

Porsh WATCH THE CORRIDOR AND SHUT THE FUCK UP! (*to Sonia*) Anything, ask me anything you like.

Sonia Let's start with a name.

Porsh Shakespeare. He's good.

Sonia They say.

Porsh And Byron.

Sonia Oh?

Porsh Attitude.

Sonia And what do you want from me?

Porsh A-levels. I know you think I'm mad but actually, I'm just good at words. Phrases. Fables. So I'll start from the beginning. My birthday. She got it wrong because I am somebody else altogether. I'm me. (*Touches head.*) In here. (*Touches heart.*) And in here. Don't you see?

Pause.

Porsh Don't you?

Pause.

Sonia I have a lot to do right now so maybe if you –

Karen Por.

Porsh See him?

Karen No, but –

Porsh Watch! (*to Sonia*) Right. Yes. Now, I know you think I'm some weird fuck-up sad desperate person come in here with a kid givin' you hard time but what I am saying is I am somebody else all together. How do I look?

Sonia Agitated.

Sonia is about to leave.

Porsh Passionate.

Sonia And I am late for a meeting.

Porsh Okay then, fast from the middle: Foster parents. The mahogany veneer cabinet, Art Deco, where I used to sit. You're confused already. This paragraph is mush.

Topic sentence. My first foster parents owned a wide variety of reference books: Phrase and Fable, Thesaurus, Etymology, usage, abusage, Shorter Oxford – that big one – grammar, syntax, tin tacks, you name it they got it and I got it from them.

The quiet in that room, just the hiss of the gas-fire, the heat. Close my eyes and smell the books, man. Pages peel sweet as skin off skin. You open the books and the world leaps right out at you. *Jumanji*!

Pause.

But the fostering was a temporary placement. So then another with no books, another with just telly, another with nothing, another with kids, another with slaps and then another and another. Eleven altogether. Well I am difficult. 'Cos my Mum died. Said she was going to work but she lied. Everything is temporary. Except words. They are stone.

Pause.

Jumanji is an average film with Robin Williams.

Sonia Your point?

Porsh Give me a chance. (*to Karen*) See him.

Karen No.

Porsh Keep looking.

Sonia Perhaps if you came back when we both have more time we could discuss an application.

Porsh It's now or nothing.

Pause. Sonia looks at the baby.

Sonia She's lovely.

Porsh He.

Sonia But he shouldn't be in this part of the college. Have you considered hairdressing? Catering? There's a crèche for students.

Porsh No.

Sonia It's okay, they all go.

Porsh I don't like it.

Sonia Trained helpers – well, training – final year NNEB –

Porsh He doesn't leave my sight ever. I want to discuss the entrance requirements.

Porsh hands over the (by now very grubby) application form. Sonia looks at it.

Sonia This stain?

Porsh You don't want to know. *(to Karen)* Kar?

Karen No.

Sonia stops reading.

Sonia Look, honey, the exam board has a computer. They have records. They check. We know if someone's trying to pull the wool over our eyes.

Porsh We?

Sonia The college. The exam board. Everybody.

Porsh Right. Big we.

Pause.

That expression . . . pull the wool – must come from wool caps innit? Middle Ages, somewhere back . . . back then when people just come along and pull them down so they can't see. Has to be. Middle Ages. Laugh a minute.

Sonia Ms Desanto, Ruth . . .

Porsh Porsh. Nickname. Which means added-on name, because in olden times people didn't have surnames they had extra names. Eke-names. Eke bein' the bit stuck on the bottom of a beehive. Who else you know knows that? I know all kind of things. Wool . . . Kar?

Karen No.

Porsh As in wool-gathering from all the little kids sent out to pick up wool from the fields and hedges an' that looked like they was just wanderin' here and there, man, but no they wasn't, they was pickin' up wool, that's what they had to do, pick up wool, and it don't come in straight lines, but don't you pick up that phone. Please! Because . . . you're a teacher, incha? And you don't know it but you have been waiting all your life for this opportunity. Give me a chance. Be the one who gives me a chance. Be that one.

Pause.

Sonia There is an access course. It's already fully subscribed for this year.

Porsh Be that one.

Karen has seen something down the corridor.

Karen It's him.

Porsh Be that one.

Karen falls back into the room.

Karen He's here.

Porsh Say it.

Karen He saw me looking.

Porsh Be that one.

Sonia But I think we can find you a place.

Porsh Thank you.

Porsh slumps in relief.

Karen Where can we go?

Porsh (*to Karen*) Stop him.

Karen How?

Porsh (*to Karen*) Tell him I'll kill him.

Sonia Who?

Porsh (*to Sonia*) Don't worry about it.

Sonia Are you in some kind of trouble? Do you need help?

Sam pushes Karen aside. Stands in the doorway.

Sam Where is he? I want my son.

Porsh stands before the buggy.

Porsh Look at me. No. Here in my eyes.

Sam Don't give me the eyes.

Porsh Do you know me?

Sam I'm takin' my son.

Porsh Would you live? I'd dig your eyes with my fork. I'd eat your cock. Don't you know that?

Sam He's mine.

Porsh No.

Sam Yes he is.

Porsh I fuck people all the time, man. Could be anybody's. Why should he be yours?

Pause.

Sam It's there in his face.

Porsh No.

Sam Let me see him again.

Porsh Best not. Be easier that way.

Sam Let me touch him.

Porsh You'll hurt him.

Sam I won't.

Porsh You will, you too rough, man.

Sam I've changed.

Porsh You're not capable.

Sam I want him.

Porsh But you can't have him.

Sam I can't just let him go. You have to listen to me or I'll do something bad.

Porsh I can handle all your badness.

Karen I'm frightened.

Porsh (*to Karen, without looking*) It'll all be over in a minute. (*to Sonia*) Take no notice of this. (*to Sam*) Just go.

Sam I'll do something.

Sonia I'm going to call the police.

Sam Who's she?

Porsh Nobody.

Sonia Oh yes, I am. I am a member of staff here and I –

Sam Member of staff? I hate members of staff!

Sam produces his knife. Sonia backs away.

Karen *Porsh*!

Porsh You can't have him, Sam.

Sam Then . . .

Porsh What?

Sam I'm . . .

Porsh Yeah?

Sam Gonna cut your head off. Either my son is given to me right now, yeah, RIGHT NOW, or . . . I cut your head off. And his head off. And my head off.

Porsh No.

Karen Please let me go.

Porsh No.

Sonia Listen –

Sam (*to Sonia*) Open your mouth again, member of staff, and this is in it.

Sonia shuts up and reaches for the phone.

Sam Touch that phone I cut your fingers off. I mean this.
(*To Porsh*) Right. Now. Let's get this clear. You and him are coming with me.

Karen Got a weak bladder.

Sam Stay where you are.

Karen Need the lav.

Porsh is facing out Sam.

Porsh Not yet, Karen.

Karen Me heart's goin'. Got a weak heart, that's why me face is red. Tell him, Porsh

Sam Is anybody listening to me?

Sonia I am going to scream.

Karen Dunt scream. Anybody fookin' screams here it's gonna be me. Me heart won't stand for this. I can feel meself gerrin' redder.

Porsh (*to Karen*) Stay calm.

Porsh still facing out Sam.

Sam Porsh?

Porsh No.

Sam Then I'll cut your head off.

Sam puts the knife to Porsh's neck. She looks him in the eye.

Sonia Oh Jesus.

Sam DON'T MOVE!

Karen Don't. Porsh.

Sonia Sweet Jesus.

Karen Don't move.

Sam (*to Sonia*) DON'T YOU MOVE! Member of staff.

Porsh swivels slowly on the blade of the knife to face Sonia.

Porsh (*to Sonia*) Access. Yes. But if I do well can I transfer to the A-level because, you see, I have always known I could do this. I'm special. My first word was helicopter. Polysyllabic. So special.

Karen FOR FOOK'S SAKE!

Sam I MEAN IT!

Porsh turns back to Sam.

What colour is he?

Porsh Still brown.

Sam How brown?

Porsh Brown enough.

Sam He don't look anythink like me then?

Porsh Got your nose.

Sam Bad luck. Say I'm his Dad.

Porsh You're his Dad.

Sam Mean it.

Porsh I mean it.

Sam Swear.

Porsh I swear.

Sam You're lying.

Porsh I don't lie.

Sam No, you're lying.

Porsh No, I don't lie.

Sam Except when you said he could have been anybody's.

Pause.

Porsh Except for then.

Pause.

Sam I'll never know now.

Porsh I'll prove it then.

Porsh takes the knife from him, and puts the baby into his arms.

Sam His Dad?

Porsh For definite. And for always. But it don't help, Sam. Because you'd only ruin him, you'd only bring him down. So you go now, please.

She takes the baby back.

You just go.

Sam goes to the door. He is almost out when he is propelled back into the room. Tommy follows with a tree support.

Sam You.

Tommy Me.

Sam How? How? You got a car. You got a car. And *I* have to wait for the *bus*. It's always the same.

Sam moves. Tommy swings wildly at him with the tree support. Sam backs away, terrified.

Tommy Don't you move.

Karen I can't take any more.

Porsh (*to Tommy*) No. Stay where you are.

Tommy keeping the tree support on Sam. Sam makes a dash for the door. Tommy drives the tree support at him but at the last millisecond rams it into the wall. Sonia is appalled.

Tommy (*to Sonia*) It's okay, I'm a doctor.

Sonia You escaped from the same place then?

Tommy No, really. (*to Sam*) This is the worst day of my life so now I am going to make it the worst day of yours.

Brandishing the tree support, he circles Sam.

He hurt you, Porsh?

Porsh No, Tommy, I hurt him.

Tommy Well, he hurt me and now I am going to hurt him too.

Karen I'm wet.

Tommy takes a wild swing at Sam. who jumps back into the room.

Pissed meself.

Sam Disgusting, man.

Karen I told you.

Tommy tries to focus on Karen's voice, but Sam makes a dash – he jumps between him and the door.

Tommy Oh no.

Karen Time to leave.

Porsh Karen, wait.

Tommy Karen?

Tommy now wants to look at Karen. He backs over to her, still keeping himself between Sam and the door. Sonia picks up the phone.

Sonia Sonia Sands, Communication, there's an intruder in here. With a knife. And somebody else with a . . .

Tommy Tree support.

Sonia A piece of wood. And a baby. That's what I said. Communication.

Karen I hate Communication, teacher got me suspended, just cause I –

Sonia Yes, Communication. Yes, a baby. So *call* the police.

Tommy drops the tree support, suddenly ignoring Sam, who takes the opportunity to rush away. He stares at Karen.

Karen (*to Porsh*) I were just going, like.

Porsh Where?

Karen Yer not me fookin' mother!

Pause.

So, yer'll be all right wi' the little lad?

Porsh Tommy . . . ?

Tommy No.

Tommy blocks her way.

Porsh Please.

He pushes Karen back into the room. A pause. Karen makes another attempt at normal exit.

Karen I won't be stopping then.

He pushes her back into the room.

Tommy (*to Sonia*) The police.

Sonia Yes.

Porsh No, Tommy.

Tommy 'She needs help.'

Porsh The police don't give help, that's your job. And she's my friend, Tommy.

Tommy All the little fuckheads in town are your friend.

Porsh You too.

Pause.

Tommy She's an immoral little cunt.

Porsh She's fourteen years old!

Tommy Then she's a fourteen-year-old immoral little cunt.

Porsh goes to her.

Porsh You don't understand.

Tommy No.

Porsh She had a plan. It just didn't work out.

Karen I were supposed to meet him under t'clock.

Porsh But he wasn't there, Tommy.

Karen And it were only two fookin' days.

Pause.

There was a little tag round her ankle.

Porsh Kelly.

Karen Kelly. And . . . she never let them tek it off. That Karen. Because it showed the baby were hers. And suddenly . . .

Porsh Don't.

Karen Sun were shinin'. And her lad'd be back home waitin', 'cos he must have missed him. And her Dad'd be on the station smilin', waitin' for her wi' social worker. Other social worker put her on the train wi' her free introductory Pampers mini-layette. And everybody looked and smiled. It were reet nice. She were reet proud. And leaned back in her seat. Wi' baby snug and snuffling against her chest. And closed her eyes. *And* . . .

Pause.

Summat happened. 'Cos when she woke up baby, she were all messy like. All like stuff on her face and up her nose and in her . . . mouth, and that. So she went to toilet wi' baby. Reet away. Get cleaned up. But first one were engaged so she had to go to next. And walkin' down corridor, all them people on the train lookin' her up and down like thinkin' who's she – who the fook's she to look after a baby – her – too young to have the mentality for it like – who's she – who the fook's she think she is? So hid in the lavvy.

Wi' baby.

In the lavvy.

But you can't stay there all day 'cause the ticket collector knocks on the door like he thought she didn't have no ticket but she had but she still had to come out to gerrit from her bag which she'd forgot and when she had the fookin' ticket he were still a cunt wi' his fookin face on him and then when he'd gone and she sat down again the eyes, the looks were worse than before 'cause of the fuss. Holdin' baby tight 'cos she were so quiet. So cold. Like. Cold.

Pause.

And just then this sign flashes past – St Albans. All bans. All the bans and nos snapped back like elastic in her eyes. What t'fook were she playin' at? Her Dad waitin' at station? That's why she come down in t'first fookin' place, 'cos she was only expecting' a paki baby just fourteen nobody knew nowt about. And here she were going back *still* fourteen to her Dad wi' her tar baby. Dreamin'. He'd flay her fookin' hide.

And all the names passin' by the train: All the bans. Hitchin.

And then she got off – that's why she got off train *after Hitchin* and hitched.

Porsh Karen.

Karen That's reet, that Karen 'cos all the signs were tellin' her what to do you see. Hitched back to London.

Pause.

T'look for her lad again.

And if it were real before, then this time it were really real. So tired. And baby crying all the time. And if they found them then there'd be what for.

Porsh Who?

Karen Police or social. And if they found them like that they'd take baby away and she couldn't bear that 'cos she had to look after baby. It were her responsibility like to look after baby come what may. And then she couldn't. She were walkin' down Oxford Street and all of a sudden she just couldn't. So she sat down against the wall and everybody walked reet past like nowt had happened. Like she were Irish. And then . . .

Pause.

And then some lad come out of that shoe shop, Shelley's in Oxford Street, so excited he couldn't wait to get his boots out and chucked the box. Dr Martens cardboard boot box was lying there on pavement telling her what to do. Dr Martens! *Doctors*, reet? *Tellin'* her . . . go back t'hospital because they know there what babies need to get them warm again. So she went. Wrapped up baby in box. Snug. Wi' tissue paper and the little tag on her ankle from when she were born in case the baby had a weak heart like her and went. And baby were safe at last.

Tommy In a bin.

Karen No. In a box.

Tommy A box in a bin.

Karen I . . . There were . . . some mistake, some like . . . bad thing.

Tommy The toilets.

Karen The hospital.

Tommy In the bin.

Karen No.

Tommy Smothered in plastic and dirty towels, all that junky slime and shit you get in a hospital toilet. Imagine.

Karen It were everything to that Karen, 'cos of its little fingers, 'cos of its heart, 'cos of her heart, 'cos of the murmur, 'cos of her Mum.

Tommy My first new life. I was so good. Beautiful. When I took her out of your body and held her in my hands. But you threw her away. And now you are going to pay.

Pause.

Sonia Anything else?

Porsh (*to Sonia*) Shakespeare. Way I see it is all the women in Shakespeare are the same, full of passion and trust, gentleness and love. Light. Never appreciated. Always misunderstood. And all the men are the same too. Quick and dark and brittle. Full of jealousy and hate.
  How's it go?

Sonia I don't . . .

Porsh The quality of mercy . . .

Sonia (*dry*) Is not strained.

Porsh It droppeth like the gentle Jew from Heaven . . .

Sonia Dew.
D-ew not Jew. Not Jew, d-ew!

Porsh There's a Jew in it, int there?

Sonia He wasn't exactly a gentle Jew.

Porsh But that's what she wanted him to be. Gentle. Like gentile. So Jew. It was obviously in his mind.

> Gentle *dew* from Heaven
> Upon the place beneath: it is twice blessed . . .
> Him that gives, and him that takes.
> 'Tis mightier than the mightiest. It becomes
> The throned monarch better than his crown . . .

Long pause as Porsh looks from one to the other. Porsh takes Karen in her arms. They move to the door.
   Tommy blocks the door. Porsh stares him down.

'S okay chicken, you're with me.

He steps aside. They walk to the door, the two girls and the buggy, the load – then Porsh stops.

(*Over her shoulder to Sonia*) Who else you know reads Shakespeare, eh? Actually, probably everybody you know reads Shakespeare.

They start to go.

Sonia September the eleventh.

Porsh stops, Karen with her.

First day.

End of play.

Discover the brightest and best in fresh theatre writing with Faber's new StageScripts

Sweetheart by Nick Grosso 0571 17967 3

Mules by Winsome Pinnock 0571 19022 7

The Wolves by Michael Punter 0571 19302 1

Gabriel by Moira Buffini 0571 19327 7

Skeleton by Tanika Gupta 0571 19339 0

The Cub by Stephanie McKnight 0571 19381 1

Fair Game by Rebecca Prichard 0571 19476 1
(a free adaptation of **Games in the Backyard** by Edna Mazya)

Crazyhorse by Parv Bancil 0571 19477 X

Sabina! by Chris Dolan 0571 19590 3

I Am Yours by Judith Thompson 0571 19612 8

Been So Long by Che Walker 0571 19650 0

Yard Gal by Rebecca Prichard 0571 1959 1

Sea Urchins by Sharman Macdonald 0571 19695 0

Twins by Maureen Lawrence 0571 20065 6

Real Classy Affair by Nick Grosso 0571 19592 X

Skinned by Abi Morgan 0571 20007 9

Down Red Lane by Kate Dean 0571 20070 2

Shang-a-Lang by Catherine Johnson 0571 20077 X

By Many Wounds by Zinni Harris 0571 20097 4

Dogs Barking by Richard Zajdlic 0571 20006 0

All Faber *StageScripts* are priced at £4.50.
If you cannot find them stocked at your local bookshop please contact Faber Sales Department on 0171 465 0045